CREATING A LIFE WORTH LIVING

VOLUME 2
UNDERSTANDING YOUR CALLING

DEBBIE N. GOLDBERG

BALBOA. PRESS
A DIVISION OF HAY HOUSE

Balboa Press books may be ordered through booksellers or by contacting:

Balboa Press
A Division of Hay House
1663 Liberty Drive
Bloomington, IN 47403
www.balboapress.com
1 (877) 407-4847

Print information available on the last page.

ISBN: 978-1-5043-5944-3 (sc)
ISBN: 978-1-5043-5945-0 (e)

Library of Congress Control Number: 2016909226

Balboa Press rev. date: 09/26/2016

This volume aids you in understanding a deeper connection to Spirit and your calling. It is focused on how to strengthen and stay steady as you continue on your journey

These books are a gift of love from Spirit. They are a guide to love, peace, purpose and healing.

These books are about undertaking a spiritual journey that will take courage, complete honesty, openness, patience, compassion, faith, persistence, and a commitment to your self to create a loving purposeful life.

These books are also dedicated to all of you, through Jesus. It is a channeled message from Jesus that needs to be heard in order for everyone to live a life worth living, a life of happiness, gratitude, love and purpose.

I pray blessings that these books bring you to a place of co-creation of your life's purpose. God – Please bestow the blessings you have bestowed onto me to the readers of these books; heal me and heal them.

Awakening from the sleep/ unconsciousness, healing and following the spiritual journey is the hardest, most rewarding and most fulfilling work I have ever done. Don't be afraid. The work you are about to do is a gift to your self and becomes much easier as you paddle down the river of life with guidance, love, passion and purpose.

Awakening to the God Within

I give myself over to my
highest, my soul,
the essence of who I am
for She is the God within.
She is who carries the light
of love, the torch,
the flame of my heart.
It is she who carries on forever,
a beautiful spirit of hope & joy,
a blessing to behold &
stand witness to all
that she stands for, divinity,
& the sacred.

Thy Will Be Done

I am dedicated to the cause
of promoting the
Reign of God within our hearts
To Love, Cherish, & Honor
Ourselves and Others

I love you and you are loved. You are looking for Love otherwise you would not have opened this book. These books teach you how to receive the most profound unconditional love and then how to give it to yourself and others.

Allow me to give you the gift of love, the secret of life and your divinity back. Walk with me through the pages of these books to find your true self and joy.

You are deeply blessed and it is time for you to collect your blessings.

Creating A Life Worth Living is a continuous series of books that build upon each other and should be read in sequence to get the most out of them.

It would be helpful to read one chapter, take time to think about the message and try to integrate it into your understanding.

Dedications, Acknowledgements, Preface & Background

In Volume 1 I acknowledged all those who have been part of my spiritual journey and who have touched these books in preparation for their release. I also included background information about myself and the circumstances that prompted me to start down my spiritual path. Please refer back to Volume 1 if you are interested in this information.

Artist's Biography

Jane Tomlinson has a Master of Art Education. She taught high school fine art for thirty-one years in the Central Bucks School District, Bucks County, Pennsylvania. Jane is retired and living in the Florida Keys. She has become a member of the Art Guild of the Purple Isles as well as the Florida Keys Council of the Arts. She is also a practicing professional photographer. Jane has worked for a local glass artist designing and creating fused dichroic glass jewelry and art pieces. She now spends her time in the Keys painting, photographing and learning about the plants that thrive in that tropical environment. She is inspired daily with the natural beauty of the Florida Keys.

About the Author

Debbie N. Goldberg has been a therapist for 18 years practicing in Pennsylvania. She specializes in mental health and substance abuse issues, providing services to adults and couples. She has worked in a variety of settings and is now in private practice, residing in Islamorada Florida. She brings the spiritual knowledge of her own awakening into her work with others to inspire healing, love, joy, purpose and creativity through their own spiritual journey.

This series of books are channeled from her own spiritual guidance and incorporates teachings from Dr. Margaret Paul's Inner Bonding Program and Dr. Barbara De Angelis' Ultimate Program.

Contents

Chapter One

Everything you need is within

❀ ❀ ❀ ❀ ❀ ❀ ❀ ❀ ❀ ❀ ❀ ❀

A gift is something you receive,
unwrap & enjoy
You are the gift explore yourself,
find your essence
and celebrate who you truly are

❀ ❀ ❀ ❀ ❀ ❀ ❀ ❀ ❀ ❀ ❀ ❀

Reaching inside of you to find all the support you need is a quest. There is more loving spiritual support available to help you evolve your soul than you could ever imagine. Look at it as having your own coaching staff with each coach focusing on teaching you a different lesson and providing you with a different type of support. Most of us don't realize that we have access to this realm, but as I stated in the first book, God's kingdom is within us, and always has been.

You will expand your ability to access this kingdom as you grow spiritually and become ready to attain the next level of consciousness. It would be too much for you to handle if everything were accessible to you all at once. It takes time to practice and integrate the knowledge and wisdom you have started to acquire.

It can be very overwhelming at first, like you are a sponge absorbing all of this new information that is completely opposite of how you have previously understood life or yourself. It will take quite a while just to integrate it all; in fact it will take a lifetime. You have to give yourself some time each day to be quiet and reflect on the wisdom you are receiving. If you don't, it will be more difficult to solidify that wisdom in your heart and put it into practice.

Your spiritual guidance and soul/spirit are always there to help you reflect on the wisdom you are learning and to help answer your questions. Ask your spiritual guidance or soul/spirit to help you find the answers that are already there inside you. It is perfectly normal to have questions and need help, since we are coming from a place controlled by our ego programing that has no awareness or insight about truth, light or love.

There will be a period of time when you will seek answers outside of yourself, and that's okay. That is why you are reading this book. We look for reassurances that we are on the right path. We find other seekers on their own journey, and it helps us feel better that we are not the only one working through this difficult process. In fact, the universe is set up to send us these reassurances and they show up at exactly the right time when needed. There are a number of fabulous programs offered around the world that can aid in raising our consciousness or spiritual journey, but not everyone has the financial resources or time to participate.

This is another reason I am writing this series of books. They can serve as a kind of self-help guide to which you can always refer whenever you might need them. Over time, you will come to realize that you never have to look outside yourself for answers since all the wisdom you'll ever need about you, your life, and purpose is already within you and readily available to you every moment of the day.

Until you become comfortable and trust the process, you will keep looking outside of you to others. At times we also resist going inside or we forget and try to do everything on our own. Remember, this is normal. Have patience with your self. There is no date by which your goal must be achieved; it is a journey.

The need to look beyond our selves for answers is all part of an important lesson...we all want immediate gratification from the outside world and we all lack trust in our selves. It is a lot to contemplate. From day one we learn to rely on others for everything. We become dependent on others for our wellbeing...emotionally, spiritually, physically, and financially. Accepting the idea that our wellbeing can be created by us and comes from within us is an extremely important shift in thinking. It can be a challenge, but it is extremely empowering.

Part of the resistance to accepting this truth is that given our ego's programing, it simply 'does not compute.' Our mind cannot grasp the deep truth of this concept. We spend so much of our time resisting things that we don't understand. We ask: "How can I stick this square peg into that round hole?" "You tell me I can do this, but I don't see how; I need to see it to believe it." Our ego programing contains a lot of black or white thinking.

We can't change our ego; it is what it is. But this leads us to the concept of faith, the fundamental, unshakable belief that there are things in the universe that cannot be proven, things so much bigger than ourselves that we cannot see or understand, and yet they do exist.

In order to feel safe, our ego mind wants control over what we think, what we believe, and how we see the world. It does this by putting everything into a context that it understands. We have all had experiences where we thought we understood something, but then discovered that we did not understand it at all. Many of us have had experiences for which there is seemingly no earthly explanation. Accepting that it doesn't know everything is a huge task for our ego. As a result our ego will resist truths if it is unable to see 'how things work.'

Journal Entry 1/17/2016
With Angel Simon

Me: There are so many things that don't make sense.

Simon: I know. It will get easier with time. The more time you spend with us the more your knowledge will grow. It is not easy being human…so many tragedies, so much drama, pain/happiness, birth, death. It is very complicated. It is important to remember not to rely on your thinking or understanding. If you consider life through a spiritual perspective it will be easier to look at everything as a planned lesson to evolve your soul. It takes lifetimes and then some. Even past prophets succumbed to the ego. It is nothing new. You do expect so very much of yourself and it continues to pressure you. **Me:** I see that I keep falling into the same trap of my patterns. **Simon:** Yes, it will stop someday soon. **Me:** I hope so, I will continue to work on staying present and connected. **Simon:** You cannot fix anyone else either Deb. They have their own process to go through. Keep focusing on yourself. Blessings are coming, miles and miles of blessings. **Me:** Thank you. Who am I talking to? **Simon:** My name is Simon. I am one of your angels. **Me:** You seem very sweet. **Simon:** Thank you. **Me:** I never heard of an angel Simon before. **Simon:** I know. There are many of us here trying to help you and everyone else. **Me:** Thank you Simon. It is interesting how Spirits take turns. I spend a lot of time with one and then someone else shows up and takes over, sort of a tag team! **Simon:** Yes. I see that is how you look at it. We all have different lessons for you so it depends on where you are at the moment, what you need and what you are ready for. **Me:** What is our time together about? **Simon**: Reflection, my love, and that can be in many ways. Like the reflection of the bible story of being human, seeing your reflection in another person and in God. **Me:** Yes, I see. What is it that you want to help me know or learn? **Simon:** It appears that you are seeing different reflections within yourself. You see your positive attributes, how capable and responsible you are, how loved you truly are and the affect you have on others. It is beautiful how loving and caring you are. You also see all of your negatives, your faults, neediness, disregarding, insecure, etc. These are reflections of your ego, your wounded selves. They have nothing to do with your soul. Only the positive attributes reflect your soul. We need to start seeing the correct perspective and not the skewed one. **Me:** How do I do this? **Simon:** By remembering who you really are. Remind yourself of how strong you are and how others see you as a positive influence. **Me:** I just had a flashback of not being that way at times. **Simon:** Remember, you are also here to teach others lessons that they need to learn also. As an example, if you lose control of your emotions and others who are struggling with this same issue see that, then you become a reflection of what they need to heal inside. This does not define you or another person. This is part of the drama of the mind, the storyline that people react to that affects them and others. So stick to reality, the truth of who you really are.

Points to Ponder

- What are the feelings you have when hearing that you have access to a spiritual kingdom within you?
- Have you read Volume 1 to understand how you can access your spiritual guide or hear your soul speak to you?
- How is your ego reacting to this information?

Chapter Two

Separation From the Ego

❀ ❀ ❀ ❀ ❀ ❀ ❀ ❀ ❀ ❀ ❀ ❀

When man undoes all that
has been given to him
Then shall he want nothing else

❀ ❀ ❀ ❀ ❀ ❀ ❀ ❀ ❀ ❀ ❀ ❀

All Souls Are To Be Set Free From The Bondage Of The Ego

The need to be able to make sense of our reality is why it is important to have a visual for your guidance if you can (I discussed in Volume 1, how we can achieve this). Having a visual experience with your guidance gives us something to hang onto. We experience it fully, visually, hearing it or knowing it in our heart. We now have a visual reference although we are not quite sure how it works, how this happens, but still, we are experiencing it.

A visual guidance helps us to begin to separate from our ego. However small that separation might be, it's a great start. Even though your ego does not want you to go inside, part of you knows that this is were you need to be and that you'll experience great love, joy, peace and contentment there. The wedge between you and your ego is now in place, which will allow you to continue to separate from your ego over time and find your soul/spirit.

Your ego will continue to try to make sense of this experience by going outside seeking information from everywhere and everything. It doesn't want to accept the truth of what part of you already knows. God/Spirit is already aware that we will do this searching. Remember, we planned our life path with God/Spirit before we were born (please see Volume 1).

The universe is set up to give us the reassurances needed to help us feel that we are on the correct path to continue our journey toward spiritual consciousness. Look at it as a treasure hunt and there are clues everywhere as to where to look or go to get closer to the treasure. That's what the reassurances are…to keep you moving forward on your journey of enlightenment.

As you do this and keep digging inward, you start to question everything you know. You start to understand that everything is an illusion and you begin to look at life differently. You ask yourself "Why didn't I see these things before?" It almost feels like magic, synchronicity, when you receive reassurances (it is all loving) and notice the small miracles happening in your life on a daily basis.

You begin to see truth in yourself and others. The truth you now see won't be the same truth you experienced before. You start to see and feel love everywhere. It's almost like falling in love with life and everyone and yourself. People smile at you that you never noticed before. Favor comes your way from everywhere, even if it is very small, little things that normally you would have not noticed. You start to shift and feel gratitude for what you are witnessing.

The only thing that has changed is you! You are waking up and because of the spiritual growth you are experiencing, it's starting to subtly change you and open your heart. It's you that is different, whether you realize it or not. As a result, you will begin to see all of the positive things happening in your life and you will affect everything around you in a more positive manner. It is an awakening, an amazing, beautiful feeling and awareness.

You will start to see that things are not just as they appear to be. You start to feel like you have some power to make things happen even though you don't understand it. It feels magical, and the magic continues to grow as you go to higher levels of consciousness. It is important to embrace all that is happening, for you are starting to see your own divinity. It is as though a window were opened just a crack, just enough to let in a small sliver of the full awakening that could possibly be in store for you.

It will take time for that window to be fully opened. Nevertheless, the glimpse you get from the opening you do see is spectacular. It fuels your passion to see and learn more, to keep digging deeper. You want to use your open heart to keep stripping away the illusion of the life that you knew and recognize that life now has a new meaning.

This is exhilarating! You now can see and understand exactly how much that God/Spirit cares for you. It brings great peace to your heart. It also begins to rock the foundation of your ego. Ego is starting to lose its power. You recognize there is something so much greater than you. You are graced with people showing up in your life, just at the right moment, spirit angels sent to help you move to the next step. Sometimes these angels are people, new acquaintances, and sometimes they are people who you now see in a completely different light who have been near you the whole time. Powerful forces are at work within the universe to lead you to your purpose. Everything is divinely planned.

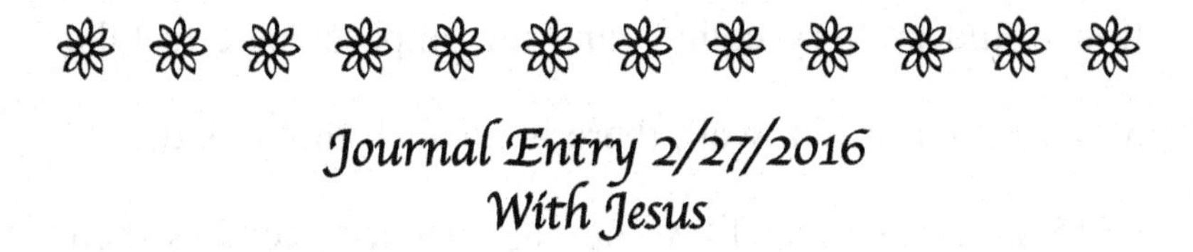

Journal Entry 2/27/2016 With Jesus

This conversation came about after my reading 'A Course in Miracles' (ACIM) and assuming from the readings that the end goal is to reach a state where we let go of all human reactions or emotions other than love or joy.

Me: So Jesus something about the Course in Miracles is bothering me; maybe I'm understanding it wrong. I know that in ACIM we are not supposed to be sad when someone dies because there is really no such thing as death. When someone losses someone dear to them how can we not be compassionate, how can we be so detached emotionally, after all we're still human? It feels callous to me not to have emotions, please help me understand this more. **Jesus:** Debbie this is a great question and I am glad you are coming inside with these questions. You are right, as a human being this would be very callous and uncompassionate to take an approach of 'Oh well, there is no such thing as death', or to say something like 'they are needed more as their spirit', or it is just their time to leave earth, or some such thing. I never meant that book to have someone be callous and forget that others are human and so are they. **Me:** I feel like we should not have any emotions at all unless it is love or joy is this wrong? **Jesus**: This is difficult to understand. As a spirit there are no emotions, just joy, well, for the most part anyway. Because you are human you are going to experience other emotions, however, the job is to detach from all of the ego emotions coming from your old programing. It does not mean that nothing will ever upset you again. **Me:** For example, say someone or my child gets hurt, it is so strange to think, 'well, that is their reality and their soul's path that is organized and planned therefore, they are not really hurt so I am not going to have any feelings about it.' **Jesus:** I understand what you are saying and you are correct, the humanness in you should have feelings, it is part of your humility of being human. To transcend all emotion other than joy and peace you would not be human anymore, that would be difficult to achieve. That is not what my expectations are for you or anyone else. That is why we are writing a simple book.

*A Course In Miracles is a book that was written by Helen Schucman in 1976. It was channeled through Jesus as a self-study curriculum for spiritual transformation. There are study groups all over the world.

Points to ponder

- Have you been practicing the guided imagery to find your guidance ('Do I have to Give Up Me to be Loved by God' by Margaret Paul, pg. 177)?
- If you have found your guidance are you having conversations with them? Can you hear your soul speaking to you?

- Are you looking for reassurances on the outside? What reassurance are you looking for and from where?
- Have you experienced any miracles that are sent to you daily? If so, what are they?

Chapter Three

The End Goal

*If you invite God to work in your heart
He will weave your soul like a fine
tapestry taking all the imperfect
threads to create a beautiful
Piece of Art*

The end goal is to align your will with God's will and to understand that you are one with God and your mutual purpose for your life. There are many starts, stops, and reversions back to old habits along this road. They are all learning lessons that will help you reach this ultimate goal.

When you begin to recognize all of the miracles in your life, it gives you a taste of what is to come. You don't mind hobbling down this spiritual road even if it is painful at times...and it is. You have to weed out all of the old programing, painful events and feelings you've experienced. You have to examine and acknowledge each one, feel the pain of them and then let them go. This means taking responsibility for all of your feelings, both negative and positive. It means that you stop blaming others, and that you forgive yourself and others. It means letting go of all of it, including attachments.

We are attached to many things that we think give us self worth. In reality, we are simply giving away our power to things or people that we think will give us self worth. Or, we are using our resentments, pain and anger to justify our behaviors. When we are able to shift our thinking from 'I need' (comfort, status, self worth) to 'I love', then we have begun to honor and appreciate our self, other people, and everything around us.

Everything that has happened to you has been your own creation, the one that you decided on before you were born, (See Volume 1, Chapter 2). I know that right now this is hard to digest, especially if you have had a lot of negative experiences in your life. Nevertheless, this is how you chose to learn the lessons for your soul's evolution.

Remember, when you made these decisions, you were your soul/spirit. As a soul/spirit we know nothing of pain or suffering. There is only love and joy and a soul knows it will never be harmed and that it does not die. When you made these decisions your soul knew you were just asleep, dreaming. Your soul understood that even though the experiences feel real, they are not.

After we were born into this world and as we grew older and experienced more of life, we began to disconnect from our soul and became attached to our ego. In doing so we forgot that we had already created a life path designed to confront us with lessons that we would need to learn in order to grow and strengthen our soul/spirit.

As you continue to grow in understanding, you will come to accept this. Right now, this may all seem very far-fetched because so many of us, including myself, carry life's battle scars from wounds that have cut and hurt us so deeply. We ask, why would I ever choose such a difficult life path for myself?

The truth is that what we are experiencing in life is actually a dream…or some of us might call it a nightmare. It is a dream that seems so very real, that takes a lot of convincing from Spirit to help us let go of the illusion that we live in reality. All that has happened has been the story in your dream, and yes it does feel real in every way, sense, shape and form. I will talk more about this in another chapter.

The spiritual road is a toll road. There are tolls that we are required to pay such as, revisiting past pain, feeling current pain, and coming to grips with all of your faulty negative thoughts and feelings produced by your ego. You either pay the toll that allows you to access your Spirit within and allows you and your Spirit to ride together to healing, or you don't pay the toll and you avoid the road altogether. Even if you choose to avoid the road right now, you will keep encountering people and experiencing events in your life that apply to the various lessons you are meant to learn.

If you are reading this book, you have decided that you are ready and willing to pay the toll and begin to explore your internal truth.

Sometimes we're not ready to travel down a particular road and it's okay to come back to that one later. Some roads are easier to walk down than others, and it is okay to start your journey by picking one of them. You have repressed your awareness of some roads, but they will appear at the right time for you when you are ready and strong enough to travel them.

As you travel down each path, you have to allow your feelings to emerge and then accept them without judgment. As you do, take your spiritual guidance with you to walk the road together and follow each feeling or belief to its origin.

Let me give you an example of one of my own journeys. I have always judged myself harshly. I have always thought that I was not good enough or didn't do enough to have someone like or love me. By the way, this is a common belief. It is irrational and untrue and comes from old programing, negative experiences and generational family transmission.

As I walked down that road to find the origin of this belief I came to understand that based on my childhood experiences, I felt that I was unworthy of love, inherently flawed and a disappointment. I felt that I couldn't do anything right to make anyone like me or make them happy. Because of these beliefs, I experienced a great deal of detachment, fear, victimization, repressed anger, loneliness, emptiness and sadness.

As I followed my feelings and thoughts I recognized that the belief that I was a disappointment to others came along with many other feelings including victimization, guilt, shame, rejection, abandonment, lack of love, sadness, aloneness and ultimately grief. I expressed all of this through anger, perfectionism issues, being a workaholic, entitlement, detachment from my self and others, control patterns, and codependent behaviors. As I grew and clung onto these patterns and beliefs, I unwittingly manipulated and controlled myself and others in order to satisfy my need for self-esteem and love. I believed that I could not trust anyone else to help me with this, that I was alone with my needs and flaws.

This pattern of thinking affected all of my relationships in that I was projecting everything about my self onto others. The pattern affected my self-esteem, my career, and blocked me from my talents and gifts because I was always deeply fearful that I would fail and be judged a disappointment or a fraud. Because we are unconscious, this is the way that many of us are living and have no idea we are doing this. We are constantly projecting everything from the past into the present.

I spent much of my life doing more than I should for others and at work (codependent behavior) in order to keep that shadow side from others and from myself. I appeared capable, strong, responsible, but I was still living and seeing out of my smallness, my ego. I didn't allow for expansion into my divinity, so whatever riches internally were there to explore and expand went unnoticed and unused until I started to do this work. I didn't recognize that the performances I was giving were also wonderful attributes of mine. I couldn't do all of those things unless they were parts of me as well.

In the first book, I talked about our energetic set point and our ego's belief system. As I began to walk down my path non-judgmentally examining my thoughts and feelings, I came to realize that my energetic set point is sadness, aloneness, emptiness, grief and misery, sometimes hyper from adrenaline and cortisol addiction. This is created by anxiety and stress. When we are stressed our bodies release adrenaline and cortisol that feels like energy, but is completely toxic to our body. We feel we can keep going, keep pushing ourselves with this energy and we do. Then we can't sleep because of these chemicals. It's a vicious addictive cycle. It kills us slowly.

When I was unconscious in my ego and alone, I was full of sadness, isolation, anger and grief. I had repressed these feelings and kept them at bay by being busy with work and trying to prove that I was not a disappointment, distancing myself from others and isolating. This was my coping mechanism for safety (although I was not unsafe). I was looking for other people and other things to fulfill my lack of love for myself. While I was engaged in my counseling practice and was helping others, I had good feelings because I was coming from a place in my heart that genuinely wanted to help others and was ultimately connected to my purpose. Yet even while I was counseling, I was essentially unaware and detached from my own self. These are all self-rejecting and self-abandoning behaviors.

For my ego, the therapist role gave me a good hiding place because it gave me a certain status and kept me enclosed in a somewhat rigid and structured environment although I lacked the awareness that this is what I was doing. I had very strong boundaries that allowed me to focus on others and detach from myself. It is interesting to now recognize that this dichotomy of helping from my heart and being detached from myself was present within me all the while.

Another important revelation was that I didn't like to be at home. As I examined that feeling more deeply, I realized that when younger, my home was the source of this energetic set point. So as an adult "Home" became a negative and scary place where I didn't feel safe, I had to stay busy all the time. Unless I was outside of home working, I was stuck in my ego, traveling down this road day after day, year after year, feeling unsafe, uncomfortable and fearful at home, and there was no truth to it!

When I looked at the rationale for my behavior, it didn't make any logical sense. At that period in my life, my home was safe. I had a loving husband. So why was I still projecting misery into my home as an adult? The answer is that the misery memory, the vibration, this energetic set point had played so long and so continually throughout my childhood, adolescent, teenage, and young adult years that it was now my set point even though my life was now totally different.

My nature is to be happy, upbeat and positive, so that's what other people saw. It was the 'acceptable' side of me that I was willing to share. I kept the shadow side of me from others and even from myself. I recognized that I needed to accept, acknowledge and feel the feelings I had as a child, understand where those feelings came from and accept that they were justified (whether rational or irrational) at the time.

I wrote in my journal and gave my "wounded children" a voice to speak all the things that they wanted to say back then but couldn't. I wrote everything I heard with no holds barred, no editing. It gave me time to sort through the feelings, thoughts and experiences so I could be compassionate towards myself and then be forgiving and let go. Journaling can be a very healing exercise in that it is very loving to your self and helpful in finding a way into your feelings and expressing them.

You are now ready to begin letting go of your feelings and stop creating experiences and reacting to them when they appear in your life.

Why don't you try this technique with one of your 'roads.' Identify a pattern that you keep seeing in yourself. This is how we learn to start taking responsibility for our feelings. I have used Margaret Paul's Inner Bonding visualization techniques (pg. 224, first paragraph- Do I Have to Give Up Me to be Loved by God?)

Points to Ponder

- Do you take responsibility for your feelings, negative and positive feelings?
- What feelings arise within you when I say you need to go back and explore painful events in your life, re-feel them, process them and forgive?
- What is your energetic set point?

Chapter Four

Revisiting Old Wounds

Bare witness to what unfolds within you
The magnificence that you are
The spark of the divine that
dances in your heart
You will forever be in awe

Dr. Margaret Paul ('Inner Bonding') and Dr. Barbara De Angelis (Making Love Work) have written programs about how to use visual imagery to accelerate healing. You use your imagination to see yourself at the age or ages when you experienced particularly painful events. Maybe you have a school picture to remind you of how you looked at that time. Use your imagination to sit and talk with your younger self. It is of the utmost importance that you approach your little self as a loving adult filled with love and compassion as you talk about past events. Imagine sitting your little self on your lap, stroking his/her hair, and expressing love so they know you are coming from a place of genuine care.

Many times we reject or dislike ourselves at certain ages because we are not seeing the truth of who we are. We are seeing our self through the eyes of our extremely judgmental ego. We need to find compassion for that child and see them through the eyes of God's/Spirit's love. There cannot be complete healing until you are able to do this.

These imagery tools are extremely useful and will lead you to healing. It is useful to have your spiritual guidance with you as you work through each visualization session. Recognizing that these wounded parts of you exist and repeatedly spending time with them will help dissipate reactions. The energy and feelings to past events that are released can be a catalyst for forgiveness.

Many people have reported feeling afraid to go inside and see what is there. This is normal, however, it is that very fear that keeps us attached to the pain. Even if you feel some fear and ambivalence, it can be of great help to take your guidance with you and ask for peace and contentment while you explore and allow your guidance to role model being loving to your little self. Keep pushing through the fears. You are only coming up against old memories of events that have already happened. You have already experienced those events and they are part of the story you created.

This work is hard, but necessary. You must honor yourself for doing this work. It is what you came here to do... evolve your soul with lessons and learn love. Remember, you are not doing this work alone. You have access to God's Kingdom within you, right at your fingertips, loving you throughout your journey.

Many of the things we are reacting to are irrational and untrue. Until we clear these beliefs and feelings we are going to struggle. Self-abandoning or denial will not work if you want to be happy and free.

You might want to take a few deep breaths right now. Take a piece of paper and write down any fears you have of going inside and healing. What might you find? What is scaring you the most?

Sometimes people will say that they don't remember much from their childhood, or that they had a great childhood. Both of these can be true, but there are usually things that we have suppressed / repressed that are driving you that are not in your awareness and need to be acknowledged.

Make a timeline with your ages on it in groups of five years. Write down all the positive and negative events that you remember. It can be something you work on for a while until you have remembered and recorded multiple events.

Look at your old school pictures or family photos to see if those images help stimulate memories. Speak with family members and ask them about special or difficult times that they remember when you were young. Your job is to uncover as much as you can. I'm sure that as you continue to work on your timeline, both good and bad memories will come flooding back.

Points to Ponder

- What do you fear the most by going inside and talking with your wounded selves?
- What did you learn about events from your timeline?
- Is there resistance to embrace and fully love any of your wounded children, teenagers or adults?

Chapter Five

The Illusion of Life

❀ ❀ ❀ ❀ ❀ ❀ ❀ ❀ ❀ ❀ ❀ ❀

We are one consciousness, one love, one energy
For always and forever
What ever you do or feel resonates
throughout the Universe
You must use your power wisely

❀ ❀ ❀ ❀ ❀ ❀ ❀ ❀ ❀ ❀ ❀ ❀

It can be unsettling to discover that all of life is an illusion. We need to realize that the truth is that everything is a reflection of you and of God's/Spirit's love and goodness. Everything is a mirror image of each other, so what you think and feel inside is what you project on the outside. If you are carrying old pain, fear, anxieties and resentments or anger this will be projected onto your world and you will continually encounter whatever you are subconsciously suppressing / repressing. The mirror imaging can create a lot of unnecessary and unwanted drama in your life. It can create painful and negative events as you let these feelings continue to fester within you.

The healing and the letting go that you need to do is absolutely critical in that it will allow you to project and consciously create the life that you want through love, peace, contentment, joy, and passionate purpose, not fear and pain.

We are all here to work through our grief and misery to attain enlightenment, forgive, love, and then to create. The creating needs to be in alignment with whatever Gods'/ Spirit's purpose is for you. As long as you continue to live life through your ego, the life that you are creating will not be in alignment with your divine purpose. That doesn't mean that you can't be successful or happy or content throughout some portions of your life. It does mean that you are not entirely in a space that will allow your soul to evolve and create the life that is your purpose on earth…to understand we came from God/Spirit and to reunite again as one to co-create.

If you can achieve this reunion, eventually you'll be able to see everything collectively as one, as the same energy, the same spirit as God. We are not just God's children; we are one with God/Spirit. Each of us is God and Goddess, masculine and feminine. It is (and we are) all one and the same.

If we all were able to recognize everyone and everything as being the spirit and energy that is God, then there would be peace in the world. I know this sounds idealistic, but this is our soul's purpose, to be a beacon of love and light and have compassion and grace for those who are still unaware and have not yet awoken.

We see a lot of tragedy in the world. Too many people are still unconsciously creating and asleep. They are suffering and in misery and are projecting that same suffering and misery energetically/vibrationally onto everyone and everything they encounter.

We can often see this in the workplace where people's negativity creates a hostile environment that results in poor morale that sucks the life and energy out of everyone. Remember, if this describes your work environment, it is mirroring you. If you are bringing any of your negative internal energy into the workplace environment, you are contributing to the problem. Each coworker is subconsciously doing the same thing. Your energy changes as you do this work and should create a different dynamic around you.

Don't expect to see a complete change in the environment. You can't make others change their projections. But you can change yours by clearing out negative thinking and replacing it with positivity, peace and contentment. By doing so, you may be able to create positive changes in the way that your co-workers interact with you. It may also be that you have to ultimately remove yourself in order to protect your new energy from that hostile environment.

I spoke before about how energy/vibration wants to harmonize with its surroundings (Barbara De Angeles – 'Soul Shifts'). If you think about it, it means that your energy can move in either a positive or a negative direction. In the wrong environment, it is easy for your newly acquired positive energy to become toxic again. How do we protect our energy? It takes time and practice.

Minimizing your interactions with sources of negative energy is a great strategy, but not always realistic. Prayer helps to cleanse our energy. Ask God to clear your energy field and fill you with love, peace and contentment. I imagine a beautiful bubble of white light that surrounds and protects me as I go through my day. Remember, you can link your imagination directly to Spirit if it is motivated by love and comes from your heart. You can also pray to have the other person's energy cleared and ask that they be filled with peace and contentment.

I realize that you might be reading this and saying how ridiculous this seems; nevertheless, it works! It isn't easy, but as you become more and more awake, you realize that the illusion of life keeps getting stripped away little by little. You begin to recognize that you have more power within you by accessing your soul/spirit and staying attached to God/Spirit. Everything around you will begin to appear magical, because it really is.

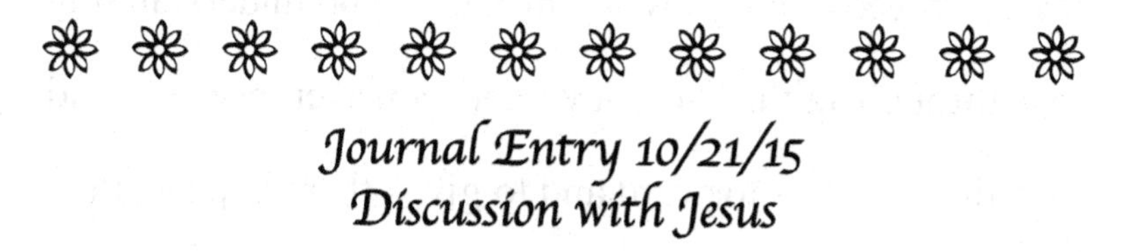

Journal Entry 10/21/15
Discussion with Jesus

Me: There has been so much awakening in me the last couple of days it is overwhelming, and trying to put the knowledge into some kind of context has been difficult. I shift from knowing to not understanding and back and forth again. **Jesus:** I know it feels like discord, you remember that is normal, it is a lot to digest. **Me:** Help me understand. **Jesus:** I will love to help you understand. I know that in the past you were not ready to hear it yet but today you understand that everything is not as it appears. **Me:** Yes. **Jesus:** It is an illusion but it is very real to you and the people around you. It is God's way of loving you, giving your spirit an experiential exercise. The purpose is to make your soul grow. We are all different aged souls and to ultimately understand is the meaning of life and love. **Me:** But so much of it is tragic. **Jesus:** Yes, but it is about taking tragedy and growing through it and understanding that through faith, trust, love and perseverance we find meaning to move forward and to give others hope so they can move forward.

Me: But we awaken to see that we have not understood the meaning of our past experience. Therefore, we remain stuck in the past with our worries and fears. **Jesus:** The awakening is to move out of that space into love and purposeful life and meaning.

* The patience given by God/Spirit is gracious and never ending.

Points to Ponder

- What are the thoughts and feelings that arise within you from hearing that everything is a mirror image of you, positive and negative?
- What have you come to understand about your own life that it is an illusion?
- How does your belief system about yourself change if you acknowledge that you are one with God?
- Have you discussed this with your own spiritual guidance or soul?

Chapter Six

Feel the Power

You are the master of your internal world
No one can do this for you
It is up to you to rise up and take on the
challenge of separating from your ego
You have all the spiritual guidance
within you to lead you
But
You are the only one that
can make this happen

We all want power over our external world. Now you are learning that you have that power, but your power to create a positive life can only come from a loving, open heart, not through fear or the manipulation of people, places and things. Love unlocks the door to everything you wish your life to be. Instead of speaking judgment, criticism, negativity or lack, we should speak love, healing, blessings and abundance for our selves and everyone else. You have the power to bless yourself and others.

We discussed before that we are one with God and that by blessing our selves and others we are shifting our lives and others in very positive directions. Try practicing this. Give it a couple of months and see the change that you create.

Sometimes you see the change immediately. You will also see that if you start projecting negative thoughts about yourself and others you will create negativity and bring it back upon yourself. It takes practice to have a conscious awareness of what is happening in your mind with thought patterns and your feelings.

Your goal is to get all of those patterns in alignment so they are resonating the same positive energy. When you notice that something is out of alignment, take deep breaths. Breathe into your heart and bring it back into a place of peace. It takes significant time to acquire the ability to keep all of our patterns consistently aligned; it is a journey. It's a difficult skill to develop since we are still constantly dealing with our ego and the realities of day-to-day life.

Ego can also trick us into thinking we are in our highest when we aren't, and that we have an open heart when we don't. Over time, you will learn how to tell the difference. You keep climbing the stairs, up and down, until you find yourself just going up.

You need to acquire and master a lot of skills just to get to this point. Your spiritual guidance will help you acquire and enhance the skills you need. Each day, I ask my guidance what I need to do, what I need to focus on, and what they want to share with me…in essence, what is your will for me today. I am always told that they want me to be happy first and that I am loved.

If you are attentive and quite, you will get constant feedback and direction throughout the day. As time goes on, you will hear that feedback more clearly. Trust your guidance. It will never steer you wrong. Even if you are hesitant, follow your guidance and see what happens. You will come to see that your guidance knows what is best for you even more that you do since you are living with your ego in charge and all of its negative programing.

Your guidance is leading you to your highest which will align your will with God/Spirit. Work on trusting your guidance. Right now, you may not be able to clearly see your life's purpose that God/Spirit and you agreed upon. It may not turn out to be what you think it is. Your purpose and expression of that purpose may be much bigger than you could ever imagine, or smaller. Either way, it still has the same value.

When you are ready, your guidance will start to prepare you. All of us are impatient and want to know what God/Spirit is calling us to do and be. This is especially true if we are older because we feel that we have wasted so much time. You haven't wasted time; you are exactly where you should be in the story of how your life is to unfold. One of my lessons is understanding that all I have to do is be happy and be myself and then everything comes in due time. This sounds simple; it's not. I have had to dismantle my belief systems and let go. It is still a work in progress, however, I've been rewarded all along the way.

We are learning to slow down and not allow self-imposed time limits and goals to dominate our lives. Ego will berate you for not mastering a certain skill yet. It will keep pushing and prodding you but all it is really doing is creating stress and taking you out of your highest. None of what the ego says is true. This work takes patience, practice, and the ability to integrate all of our newly acquired knowledge into our daily lives.

Break the chains of programing by being loving to yourself. Do the work that needs to be done. It is as though you are just starting to understand how to play the piano.

You can't expect to become a concert pianist overnight. It takes long, hard work. You can't force it to happen quickly. Don't listen to your ego and expend energy when you hear ego judging you. Ignore it. Ego knows absolutely nothing of the truth about you or anything else.

Points to Ponder

- If you had to put a percentage of how open or closed your heart is, what would it be?
- Are you trying to control your external world? Is it working?
- Try blessing yourself and others throughout the day and see what happens.

I am a blessing, I am blessed

God, please bestow the blessings you have blessed upon me to _____ (fill in the blank) heal me and heal ______(fill in the blank).

I also love the Ho'oponopono Prayer which is an ancient Hawaiian practice of reconciliation and forgiveness (Wikipedia definition). Use this when you feel that you are wronged by someone or had negative thoughts about someone. You can say it to yourself or out loud.

Please forgive me

I'm so sorry

I love you

Thank you

Chapter Seven

Let It Be

Being honest and true to
yourself is how you become
A blessing to others

It is important to accept where we are and what is happening in our lives. When we resist, we are unnecessarily expending emotional energy. We waste so much energy day in and day out that it dims our light within. As we have seen, that energy could be put to far more useful and creative purposes. Resistance causes stress and creates a toxic environment, physically, emotionally and spiritually.

Now think about what experiences in your life you have been resisting since the time of your earliest memories. Everyone has experienced some kind of trauma, whether large or small. Many of us struggle with past trauma that have left us feeling hurt, flawed, unloved, abandoned, rejected, alone. We don't know how to let go of past pain. Our ego lives in that world of past pain. It also lives in the feeling that we need to constantly worry and strategize how to protect ourselves from any kind of pain or suffering. Ego thinks it knows what will keep you safe, but it's all irrational and untrue and keeps you living in fear.

When we wallow in the past and the programing associated with it we can't heal, we just keep projecting it into our life. We resist letting go and feel justified in blaming our selves and others for past pain and trauma. Our inability to let go of the past keeps us from being present. Why do we resist letting go? Why don't we just accept what is or what was?

We resist because we don't want to take responsibility for our feelings, and don't know how to process our pain. We don't see how these past negative experiences fit into our bigger picture. Remember, before we were born we picked our life's path. We chose the people and experiences that we would encounter. When we chose this path we didn't understand pain and misery. As a soul/spirit we didn't experience these things. But the soul's goal is to evolve its consciousness to a higher level and, unfortunately, that evolution can only come from witnessing the suffering and misery.

If you never experienced any trauma or suffering you would probably not be reading this book right now. You wouldn't be trying to learn how to evolve and transcend the suffering, how to align yourself with God/ Spirit, how to find your gifts and express and them in a way that is in accord with your true purpose. Like everything else, this takes time to digest.

My early years were filled with pain. I experienced a lot of trauma from emotional, physical, and sexual abuse.

I spent much of my life being angry and building an invisible shield of armor (my ego) so that I could avoid pain. In reality, that armor (putting a cement wall around my heart) caused more pain. I never recognized that my armor was the cause of the pain I was experiencing until I started to do this work.

My armor stopped the flow of love coming into and going out of my heart. Even though I felt so much love in my heart for my children and others, they never got to feel the depth of that love. Instead, what they experienced was all of my fears and my negative programing projected onto them. They received only the smallest sliver of the love I felt for them.

I eventually came to see that I had a lot of repressed self-hatred at different stages in my life and withheld love from my self and others. As my children reached those same ages, I unknowingly projected all of that negative energy on to them, which was mostly fear and control. I passed on to them all that I had not healed, and they reacted accordingly.

This happened because I was living unconsciously and not having any awareness of what was truly happening within me. As we all have, I had received generations of emotional baggage and programing passed on to me. My children were not just getting my baggage and programing, they were getting the whole negative and positive multi-generational package. I also know I passed on many wonderful attributes to my children as well. It all gets mixed into the pot of who we are. It's all part of the fabric of our ego. We are all recipients; it is generationally transmitted.

Maybe you see your children on a wrong path…acting out and behaving in ways that trigger all your fears and anger. If so, it's because you haven't yet dealt with your own traumas, belief systems and pain. Your children will receive your energy and will act it out in their own lives and within their own families unless we (and they) do the work of recognizing and letting go. If you are able to recognize, acknowledge and heal all of your feelings and pain, your children will be able to do so as well. You can change their energy to love, openness, and acceptance by changing yours.

Points to Ponder

- Are you expending unnecessary energy by constantly trying to make sense of past hurtful or negative experiences or trying to control your external life or your future?
- How have you been processing your pain?
- Do you see your children's behavior as reflecting the mess you are inside of you?
- What walls have you built around your heart?
- What has been negatively and positively generationally transmitted from your own family? Anxiety, scarcity, fear, depression, substance abuse, poor relationships, anger?

Chapter Eight

Let It Go

❀ ❀ ❀ ❀ ❀ ❀ ❀ ❀ ❀ ❀ ❀ ❀

There once was a young prince in Egypt,
Who loved to play outside in the sun
His heart filled with joy just from taking
in the radiance of light and feeling loved.
He believed that this light was the
source of everything good and alive.
He nourished himself in this light everyday
as much as he could knowing that someday
he will not have this opportunity.
He believed there would come a day that
he no longer would see the sun. He didn't
realize that the sun and it's radiance is
connected to something so much bigger and
that the radiance was actually within him.
Upon his death he recognized that
all of that light and love was already

within him, that the sun was just a reflection of him, his life force.

We need to let go of everything. We need to release the programing, the pain, the belief systems, the story… whatever is holding us back. It isn't easy getting to the necessary level of acceptance and acquiring the ability to honor others for the role they played in your life to help you evolve your soul. They played their part in your story and did their best to help your soul evolve, just as you did in the part that you played in their story/ life. Forgiveness, acceptance, and letting go takes time. Once you attain that stage, you are free.

Your ego's sole purpose is to avoid pain and receive love. It has been trying to understand the purpose of the misery you have suffered, but it can never do so. Your ego is irrational, does not understand truth, take blame/ responsibility, and does not believe in anything spiritual, so there cannot be any real understanding. This is what the resistance is all about; we rebel. We feel justified in holding on, as it is righteous indignation and we feel it gives us power or leverage over someone else. As far as your ego is concerned, all of the misery you have suffered simply does not compute.

As you continue to grow spiritually, you'll be able to understand the purpose of your past suffering. It was purposeful and was a necessary catalyst to help you to learn your soul's lessons. However, there is no need to keep hanging onto the suffering like your favorite pair of jeans that you can't throw away. We need to create space inside of our selves by letting go of everything. This space allows all the talent and purpose within you to come out. Everyone who played a role in helping you learn those lessons should be celebrated, even those who were the cause of so much of the pain and suffering. Those people were simply playing the part you assigned to them.

As your soul grows, it becomes easier to see everyone in your life as a miracle and a blessing, and to understand that you are a blessing in their lives as well. You may not see it, but you are helping others to learn their lessons. When we transcend, the love and light we project helps take others to a higher level of understanding. We are all teachers in a sense, including you.

Moving beyond all the misery allows you to live from your heart and create a safe and loving vibration for yourself. It also encourages others to be in harmony with you and to grow within themselves. When you discover your gifts, you will bring enlightenment and love to others, no matter how your gifts and talents are expressed. The expression of your gifts will come from your soul and our soul speaks to other souls.

Since we are all on different paths and are at different levels of consciousness, the expression of our gifts will be geared to multiple levels of understanding. Your guidance will help you understand this. No gift, or expression of a gift, is more important than another.

One of the most difficult challenges we face as we practice letting go of our pain and misery is gaining the ability to see everyone we encounter as special and a miracle. Contrary to what our ego tells us, no one is better than another. No one rates higher than another. It is only our ego that needs to place everyone in a hierarchy of importance. This comes from our smallness, not from our highest. God loves and values you just as much as me. Each of us needs to love and value others as much as we love and value ourselves.

This is where we get caught up in so many relationship struggles. You can only love someone else as much or as well as you love your self. Our ego will often pretend to show love and honor for others in an effort to gain love and acceptance for itself. When we transcend and can love our selves fully, we can then love others fully. We can accept and honor their humanity and our own. This is what sets us free from the chains of living in fear and alone.

Points to Ponder

- How are you at letting go of past and current hurts, irritations, annoyances?
- What holds you back from letting go? Do you ruminate over hurts or suppress them?
- How do you look at the people who hurt you in your life? When I talk about looking at them as a blessing, how do you feel?

Chapter Nine

Forgive, Forgive, Forgive

❀ ❀ ❀ ❀ ❀ ❀ ❀ ❀ ❀ ❀ ❀ ❀

Our journey is about growing our heart
It is the only thing that matters

❀ ❀ ❀ ❀ ❀ ❀ ❀ ❀ ❀ ❀ ❀ ❀

We need to forgive our selves and others for not being perfect. Not forgiving is poison to our soul. Forgiveness melts our heart and expands it. Holding a grudge just suffocates us with poison, contracts our heart. When our heart contracts everyone around is negatively affected.

When we turn away from forgiveness we are looking for validation or revenge and neither works. We become toxic, whether we see it or not. There's no real justification for failing to forgive. It changes nothing. It can't change whatever happened, or whatever event occurred that caused our hurt and pain.

We try to attain perfection when really as humans there is no such thing. As a soul, we are already perfect; we are not broken. Our ego looks at our life's experiences and believes that we're broken and need to be fixed. Our ego blames others for the brokenness that it thinks it sees. With our ego in charge, we then try to fix others because we see them as broken. In truth, we are actually only seeing a reflection of ourselves.

We don't need to be fixed; we need to be healed from the belief that we are broken and flawed in the first place, or that others are broken as well. We need to accept our feelings and be compassionate and loving towards them in order to heal them. Having feelings of hurt, sadness or anger does not mean we are broken. When we take responsibility to heal our wounds with love and compassion then we can release and let go of them.

This is a difficult concept but I am going to try to explain it as best I can based on a thought that came to me recently during a meditation.

Because we have labeled traits, feelings, form and everything else as good or bad, negative or positive, pretty or ugly and so on we are assigning these labels to different parts of us whether it would be body image, thoughts, feelings or behaviors. At the end of this chapter I've written a quote about this level of consciousness.

Due to this labeling we are causing separation within us, such as: this part of me is good or this part is bad, this is acceptable and this is not. Think of a prism and visualize that each facet is holding or reflecting a separate part of us we have deemed good or bad. We have tolerance for certain facets and not for others based upon what our ego tells us as well as on what we have 'learned' from our programing. Our job is to stop assigning labels to these facets and accept the prism as a whole. That whole piece of glass is perfect with everything in it, no matter what it is. All facets in the prism combine to make the whole, and this is the perfection.

For myself, my prism facets would include my soul, a sad part of me, a happy side, a vulnerable side, a fiery side, a responsible side, very focused, unfocused, irresponsible side, a funny side, a serious side, independent, dependent, my ego, etc.

Most of us are looking for perfection or only seeing ourselves worthy if the whole prism is reflecting only good or positive things, acceptable traits we learned from society. This will never happen because we are human and using an illusion to rate ourselves. The point is that the prism is already perfect, even with the dichotomy of all the different facets of us. It gives us depth and makes us who we are.

The pressure and stress of creating and maintaining an illusion to hide what we deem as negative is killing us. You can see how this gets projected out into society when we are not tolerant of certain parts of us that do not fit into what we think of as mainstream society, what is acceptable…what we look like, what our job is, our age, disabilities, performance, abilities, etc. And then we throw in our ego with its faulty belief system and we are a mess inside. We are then creating this same mess on the outside.

Seeing each of the many facets of our self as being separate and distinct, some of which are good and others bad, causes us to react internally/externally in anger, aggression, judgment, passivity, avoidance, control, self destruction, passive compliance, anxiety, depression, apathy, etc. We are acting out of the intolerance we have for our own self. This is why there is so much hatred and anger in the world. Too many of us do not accept that we are perfect just the way we are, flaws and all. If we cannot accept ourselves how can we accept others or have tolerance for those that we see as being different from us? We are projecting our ego's perception of our own ugliness out into the world.

To add more complexity to this, the prism also contains the past, present and future, and they are all happening simultaneously. This is why all of the past hurts feel like they happened just yesterday. It is also why we sometimes get glimpses into the future. I will discuss this more in another chapter.

None of us are broken. If you can see this, you have achieved a huge shift in your thinking. We spend so much time outside of ourselves looking to fix our selves or blame others because we are unable to see our own perfection. We try to achieve perfection in the way we look or perform, in how much money or material things we have. We chase the career that will give us status. We look for love and acceptance outside of our selves. Even when we attain high levels of achievement and success we feel as though there is still something missing. We don't know the truth of who we already are. Our job is to connect to the highest part of our selves. That is where the perfection lies, in the God within and this is a facet in our prism.

It is extremely difficult these days to find quiet time with all of the technology, all of the noise around us, the incessant chatter inside us. Modern life connects us to all sorts of information but at the same time it disconnects us from our true selves. If we are unable to connect to our own truth then we can never be connected to anyone else. We become so disconnected from our spirit/soul we can't even see truth.

Of course, our ego believes that it knows the truth, but it doesn't and never will. What we are feeling is not being connected to our selves or anyone, and this feels like sadness, aloneness and grief. This is why we hold onto material things; we collect 'stuff'; we collect people.

Most of the clients and couples I work with suffer from this disconnectedness. It is very lonely and it's a shame because everyone tries so hard to be connected to someone or something. We bend over backwards to make people happy or to fit in so that we can feel love and accepted. But ultimately, we have a fear of intimacy. It is a fear brought about by our failure or inability to trust our selves, God, anyone or anything. We spend so much time guarding and judging our selves, we don't know how to let our selves, God or anyone else into our hearts.

Our souls/spirit are all inherently intuitive. When our soul speaks to us we often say that we have a 'gut reaction' to something. Most of us don't listen to our intuition/soul, our own truth, because we don't trust ourselves. We look to others to tell us what is right or wrong, good or bad. Other times we are too stubborn to listen to our inner guidance, or anyone else for that matter.

As humans, we find countless reasons not to become quiet, to go inside our selves and listen to our hearts. We need to become more lighthearted and learn to forgive our selves and others for not meeting our expectations of perfection and love.

It is difficult to come to terms with the fact that part of you thinks and feels broken (ego) while another part of you is happy and knows it is just fine (soul/spirit). When we give our ego a voice, we act as if we were broken, or hide the fact that we believe that we're broken. When we live in our ego, all we see is brokenness everywhere. We then contribute to that perception from our own negative thinking and energy. We make the world a self-fulfilling prophecy.

Remember, we are manifesting whatever it is we believe and feel about ourselves. If we think we are broken, we will be. The manifestation of our negative thoughts and feelings is a huge problem. Our ego is always projecting fear, scarcity, victimization, negativity and brokenness into our lives.

The more work you are able to do to separate your self from your ego (not listening to it or giving it any power) and see ego for what it really is it will help you temper all of the negative manifestations around you. If you keep working at it, eventually your positive thinking and creating will take over. This takes enormous discipline in a much different way than what we are used to.

As you are progressing along your path, the changes will be very subtle at first. Even though it may not be readily apparent to you, you are making amazing advances. We are all so programed to only recognize immediate gratification that we don't see the progress we are making over time; but it is happening. The more time you can set aside to be by yourself and integrate all you have learned, you will be amazed by all of the wisdom you have acquired and the positive changes you have already made.

Points to Ponder

- Who needs to be forgiven but you are holding them hostage instead, blaming them for how you feel?
- Do you see yourself or others as broken?
- If you drew a prism on paper with all the different facets, what would you put in each one of those facets that make up you? Can you see the separation within yourself of what you deem as good or bad?

In the mirror of life we see the illusion of who we are and it takes time to stop allowing the illusion to define us, for we are all so much more. The illusion we see is of all the fractured broken parts of us that need to be healed, the parts that guide our days and nights. Every now and then we see through another lens, another pane of glass, and we see all the amazing and loving parts of us that are already perfect, it is our soul, our heart. This is a window through which we can see our truth and our divinity. Taking time to look and explore the dichotomy that lives within us is our life's journey, to accept and have tolerance for that dichotomy, and to heal the fracture in the glass that keeps up separate, blending into one with our highest self.

Chapter Ten

Projecting Positive Energy for the Planet

*If self-love were inherent in everyone
then our planet would look very different.
All souls need to move towards self-love*

None of us can deny that the external world is in a sad state of affairs. The human condition can be heartbreaking and unfair. Most of the world isn't doing the necessary spiritual work and as a result, ego, greed, fear and hatred are in control. Each day we witness a collective anger, hatred, and lack of compassion for our selves and others within and without.

Every human being is here to do the same thing, to transcend and evolve her/his soul. Each of us has the responsibility to do this. If we continue to pass on generation after generation of unhealed family anger, victimization, entitlement, hatred, scarcity, fears and frustration, then we are collectively adding to all the negative energy in the world.

Some people have grown up with more education and opportunity than others. It is important to help people improve their condition as opposed to pushing them down. We need to pull others up with us. We exert a positive influence by doing our own spiritual work and by creating and passing along love, encouragement and positive energy. If we allow scarcity, discrimination, victimization, entitlement, judgment, anger, and hate to dictate our lives, then that is what we will continue to create for our selves and for others.

This is all part of our soul's lessons. We all have the power to heal ourselves by transcending our ego. We recognize that ego will always be a part of us, but we refuse to give it power. As we do this we then have power to help others heal and evolve. Our positive energy and our love are contagious. This is our role as humans, to do our spiritual work and evolve our souls, grow our hearts.

Sometimes we become so upset with the injustice we see that our energy turns negative even though our intentions are in the right place. Since we are projecting all of the unresolved unfairness that we experienced in our life, when we encounter injustice, we react to it with anger, judgment and hatred. All we're really doing is creating more negative energy. What is required is that we react to injustice and misfortune with compassion and love and have grace by praying for people to heal and attain more light (wisdom).

If we are coming from a standpoint of not understanding life and projecting negativity, anger, and frustration, then we are unwittingly participating in the destruction of our selves, others, and the planet. It is all vibrational energy

(Barbara De Angeles). If that's the case, then forgiving our selves and others for our lack of understanding can aid in making positive changes.

The ego is ignorant of all things within and without. To expect others to 'just know' what is right or wrong comes from our ego's ignorance. When we expect others to act in certain ways we believe that we are somehow better than they are, and we are not. No one is better than another. We are all the same. Some of us have a little more knowledge. Some of us have better opportunities. It's easy for our ego to give us a feeling that we are entitled, but we are not. This is all a lack of maturity, blaming others for our pain and suffering. The ego is extremely immature.

As you grow in understanding, you realize that your soul is already perfect and that as your faith and trust increase, you will be blessed with the abundant life you deserve. Your blessing isn't in the future; you have already been blessed. It is a part of your divinity and your journey. You don't need to worry about anything. It is all waiting for you. You simply need to keep digging inside to find it, see it, know it, and then consciously co-create it.

We still have to live in the natural world where we have no control over others, just our selves. If something doesn't work out, then it was not meant to be. If a door closes, another will open. We simply have to be open, patient and willing to receive. As you continue to evolve, your alignment with God / Spirit will bring you into alignment with what's best for you and the universe serves it to you on a silver platter, it just comes to you at exactly the right time.

Continue to dream and create. Hold a vision of your dream and write it down. Set a goal date for when things will be expected to happen and use your guidance to help you with this. Hold the vision, but let go of the outcome. Hold the vision in your heart, but allow faith and trust to lead the way. Your vision will manifest when you are ready for it. Include a loving peaceful vision for the planet as well.

Don't consciously try to push your vision forward too quickly. When you do and the time isn't right, you'll get a lot of resistance from the universe. Your vision will manifest at the most perfect time and it will be amazing.

Remember, part of evolving is learning to have trust and faith in God/Spirit and in your self. No dream is too big, so envision and create the life you want. Visualize yourself, centered, evolved, living from your heart, full of love for yourself and others. Visualize (but not in your ego) how others will feel about you. See how you are expressing your purpose in life, if you can, and how you add to the collective consciousness of the world. What does your life look like? What does a day in your life look like? Remember, life is an illusion and although we have awakened spiritually, it is time to make a new story that is devoid of all the old programming and patterns from the last story. Make it a good one.

Points to Ponder

- What is your worldview? How do you see your role in the world?
- What thoughts or feelings do you have when I say that what you do affects the world at large?
- Are you interested in doing this work for yourself knowing it will have a major impact on your family and your world?

Chapter Eleven

How Do You Find the Dream in Your Heart?

❀ ❀ ❀ ❀ ❀ ❀ ❀ ❀ ❀ ❀ ❀ ❀

Have peace within you
That is all that matters

God /Spirit has placed a dream, a purpose, a passion in the heart of each of us. Our dream is connected to our purpose and God's will. As you begin to create your dream life, your new life story, it's necessary to find and include the dream in your heart.

As you meditate or pray, it's important to ask God/ Spirit to show you the dream in your heart or your purpose. Allow God/Spirit to speak to you through thoughts, images, inner hearing, or just knowing. Keep focusing until you have your answer. It may not come right away. It may not come all at once. When your dream does appear, you might be surprised to find that it is very different than what you originally thought it would be. So, be prepared for anything.

Once you understand your dream/purpose, you may realize that you have a lot of hard work ahead of you. You might have to go back to school to enhance or acquire some new skill. You might need to become proficient in doing something that has always terrified you before, such as public speaking. That would be me!

Be open and receptive to what you hear. Your ego may not agree and become judgmental about your dream/purpose. Your ego may feel threatened when it realizes that achieving your dream will mean ego's loss of control over you. It may fill you with fears and self-doubts.

Just observe the ego and don't let it interfere with following through. Over time you'll learn to trust your guidance more than your ego. You never have to protect yourself from your guidance, but you'll always need to protect your mind and heart from your ego.

Have you ever had a dream of what you really feel passionate about? Did achieving the dream seem impossible, so you dismissed it and forgot about it? Take out a piece of paper and go back as far as you can remember and write down any memories of dreams that you had in your heart, even if they seem silly to you now. Ask your guidance the truth about these dreams and whether they are in alignment with the dream/purpose that God/Spirit put in your heart.

If you can't find any memories, right now, don't worry, try again later. Your guidance will bring those memories to you when you are ready to know and receive them. Sometimes we think we're ready to receive something and we're anxious and impatient to take the next step, but we're really not quite ready yet. When we're impatient with our journey's progress (or perceived lack thereof) it's a sign that we need a little more grace for our process. Learning how to enjoy the process and not just get to the destination is part of our lessons. It is one that I struggle with myself. I have always been focused on the destination and missed all the life and enjoyment in between. We're always impatient, always pushing the process according to our own time line. Impatience comes from our ego. Breathe, relax, be patient and forgiving. Your new story is on its way.

If you're not getting answers yet, it's okay. It just means more work needs to be done before it will be revealed to you. Don't become frustrated. We're always trying to push the future for reassurance. We dislike not knowing what will be happening next or not having control over situations. We just need to stay in the present so we can continue to grow. It may be that you're acquiring wisdom that is needed before you can fully understand your purpose. When it is the right time and you have your answer you will then mold it into your creation dream.

See yourself living your creation dream and see it having a successful outcome. See your dream and feel it in your heart; it needs to be congruent with all parts of you. It's your heart's desire to express your dream for the greater good…the collective good of all.

I remember being about nine years old and telling God that I want to be one of his angels so I could help Him help others. I distinctly remember saying this repeatedly around that age. I remember feeling like I was a bad girl. I used to lie a lot and was mischievous. I told God that I didn't want to be that person anymore. My experience of God felt fatherly because I needed a strong loving father role model. Our connection with Spirit comes in whatever form we need and whatever form we will accept to help nurture, love and heal us, although, God is energy not form.

I always knew God was there with me even though I had no formal religious teaching or upbringing. I had an angel with me then who would hold me and comfort me as a child. Over time and growing up in difficult circumstances, I forgot and became disconnected from hearing and seeing him. Even though I had become disconnected, my inner guidance never abandoned me, just as it will never abandon you. And even though I had turned away, my intuition caused me to feel that I was still being led by some positive energy.

I didn't reconnect with my spiritual guidance again until I was fifty-six. I could see, hear, and feel Jesus. It was a huge surprise for me that Jesus was my guidance. Being Jewish, I didn't understand how that could be and went through a process of having to undo my societal programing in order to just accept love and not question the source.

Jesus is a master teacher in God's Kingdom. It is a great comfort to know His love and wisdom. He saved my life. I couldn't imagine going through the rest of my life without Him being with me every moment of every day. I learned that we are all given the love and support we need and that gift has absolutely nothing to do with religion; it is all divine love and light and there are many spiritual guides waiting to share love and wisdom with you. As my own spiritual practice grew through taking a 30-day course with Margaret Paul to raise my vibration, I was then able to see and hear God, my Higher Self, my Older Wiser Self, Archangel Michael, my father who passed away in 2008, my maternal great-grandmother and others. It has been a blessing and changed my life.

You will feel the same way when you find your spiritual guidance. Your guidance will know what and when is best for you. With the support you receive you can flourish and become the person you are meant to be. That is your guidance's goal for you. Your guidance will give you all of the love, direction, reassurance and patience that you need along the way. It's a pity we don't understand that we have access to these gifts all of our lives. But then again, if you truly understood who you are from the very beginning, it would not make your awakening as wonderful an experience as it's going to be.

Points to Ponder

- Have you tried asking questions to your spiritual guidance about your purpose or dream that you have to fulfill?
- Is there something you have been dreaming about doing in the future?
- How does time affect whether you think you are making progress or not?
- If you are struggling with knowing a dream or a purpose, try to create an end product of what you would feel like achieving a life dream or purpose. Visualize what you would feel like, look like, how would others respond to you?
- Have you used the tools in Margaret Paul's book to access your guidance? If not, why?

Chapter Twelve

Putting God/Spirit First

❀ ❀ ❀ ❀ ❀ ❀ ❀ ❀ ❀ ❀ ❀ ❀

My heart feels full with God's
glory, it is deep within me
It washes over me with peaceful contentment
and bliss, knowing that He is in control
of my life, that I need not worry
And if I should fall, He is always
there to catch me, to lift me up to my
highest and bring me out of the dark
which is where my mind longs to go.
He sees the beauty in me when
I can no longer see.
I rest my head on His chest
and He consoles me

I humbly accept His hand for there is no
other love that can fill as completely and fully
I am your humble servant forever more

There are a lot of misconceptions surrounding the concept of putting God/Spirit first in our lives. Most religions teach that you need to do certain things and live certain ways in order to put God first. This can be very confusing. I am writing from a spiritual standpoint, not religious. We are all spiritual beings first and foremost.

Since we are all spiritual beings created from God's/Spirits mind, love and energy, we all have the same goal of evolving our soul to a higher level of consciousness and growing and opening our hearts. Putting God first means putting your self first. This is the complete opposite of what most religions or programming will tell you. None of the major religious theologies teach that we should put our selves first. That is why most people believe that if we do think about ourselves first, we are being selfish. This idea of selfishness is one of our ego's most powerful tactics to prevent us from caring for ourselves spiritually, emotionally and physically.

Let me clarify, God/Spirit wants what is best for you and knows you better than you know yourself. God/Spirit created you with a special purpose, gifts, and talents. Unless you develop an intimate relationship with God/Spirit (which is also within you as your higher self) you cannot know what is best for you or what you were created for to do. So having a relationship with God is indispensible to knowing who you are, what your purpose is, and understanding the best way to take care of your self in all areas of your life. God/Spirit holds the keys to unlock everything you need to know about life. There is nothing special that one has to do, say, or be. All you need to do is open your heart and tell God/Spirit that you want a relationship so that you can fully understand you. That's it.

Some religions refer to this as surrendering. Most of us don't even think about surrendering until we're completely beaten down, desperate, despairing, and without hope. We've hit rock bottom. We're cornered and see no other way to turn. We surrender.

We don't have to wait to surrender to God/Spirit until we're filled with misery or illness. Most of us resist the idea of surrendering because our ego believes that by doing so we are giving up our life and our power. There's no truth to this.

It is our ego that fears giving its power to anyone or anything. If you believe there is nothing more powerful than you, that you can find all the answers and figure it all out, then you are living in your ego. Remember, it's your life's journey to stop living in your ego and get in touch with your spirit/soul.

If you have a sense that you have a higher part of you or know there is a better part of you somewhere deep inside, then you have identified your spirit/soul. The only way to evolve that highest part of you is to nurture this connection and become one again. This is the part of you that is created by God/Spirit.

Your spirit/soul is pure love, light, compassion and regard for you and everything else. It doesn't judge. It is filled with grace and understanding that you are human and asks nothing in return other than you accept all the gifts that are waiting for you. These gifts are love, peace, wisdom, knowledge, and truth. They are wrapped in enough love and patience to allow you to take as much time as you need to understand them and integrate them into your being.

As you work your way through this process of connecting to your spirit/soul, you are subtly evolving into who you truly are and are coming into the life and happiness you deserve. The journey brings you freedom from all worries and fear. Know that you are taken care of forever.

Journal Entry 1/10/2016
With Angel Simon

Simon: God's purpose is to heal everyone through the blessing of His love, His spiritual kingdom that is always there to help us heal and gain all that He has given us inside and outside of us, past, present and future. You are beginning to understand. Now you need to let it sink in as you dwell on this, and allow it to be your own understanding of human life. The meaning is to heal your human hurts which allows your soul to evolve to its highest. You are God's progeny. **Me:** What is progeny? **Simon:** Lets look it up. **Me:** (I get told to look up words and concepts all the time) Progeny is a descendent or descendants, offspring or offspring collectively. So we are all God's offspring (human life and all that exists) and the meaning of our time on earth is to find God, remember that we are connected to Him, that we are His offspring and that we come back to Him as our parent to heal us by awakening to all the love He is surrounding us with. We have to recognize that we have become closed off to our soul/spirit in a kind of a "great sleep". We have to awaken and allow God to re-parent us through His love so that we can mature into our divine soul, our highest. He is our soul's mom and dad, God's soul made our soul. Our soul needs to be nourished and that spiritual nourishment can only come from our spiritual parent. So God represents our mom and dad as a human way of looking at it and God is both male and female, yin and yang, the flow of energy, a life force, like the sun. **Simon:** Yes, very good. **Me:** So why do I experience God as a male? **Simon:** Some of it is social context, programing, some that you needed to heal paternal wounds and remember that even though you received those wounds from your father, you also experienced love from him as well. **Me:** So, God is experienced through whatever a person needs, whatever a person feels comfortable with. **Simon:** Yes, but God is neither male nor female; He is energy, He encompasses both. **Me:** We all like symbolism, so if I were to see God as energy what would it look like? **Simon:** Everything, God is your blanket or the TV or your coffee cup, your husband, children and yes, yourself. **Me:** Wow, that's really a lot to take in. **Simon:** Symbolism is very important, that is why God sent Jesus, saints, apostles, so that there is a symbolic reference to what God is. Humans relate to symbolism and the symbols are there to remind people to wake up from the great sleep and reconnect to their soul's purpose in life, to mature and grow, just like you do…like a child growing into an adult. But only God can mature and parent your soul.

Points to Ponder

- Take out some paper and write down what your programing has been saying to you about what it means to put your self first. What has it been telling you about surrendering to God/Spirit?
- Ask yourself what is blocking you from developing a personal relationship with God/Spirit, the highest part of you. What can you do to remove some of the barriers? What keeps you from letting go or believing in something greater than yourself?

Chapter Thirteen

Why Do We Call God, God?

❀ ❀ ❀ ❀ ❀ ❀ ❀ ❀ ❀ ❀ ❀ ❀

When the willows blow in the
wind the seeds are carried away
and deposited along the way.
These seeds are new life beginning
to take hold and become a beautiful
expression of nature.

❀ ❀ ❀ ❀ ❀ ❀ ❀ ❀ ❀ ❀ ❀ ❀

I don't profess to be a student of linguistics. I have made no study of languages and how they have developed and changed over time. I subscribe to a translation of the English word 'God' suggested by Craig Bluemel in his article 'The origin of the English Word for God', Part One, which can be found at Bibleanswerstand.org. Bluemel suggests that the English word 'God' translates from another language where the word means 'good.' The word 'God' stands for 'divine good' or 'involved one."

My definition of the word 'God' for this book is 'divine being of good'. I see God as energy, divine spiritual energy. I think it is easier for others to accept the idea that we are all 'divine beings of good', that we are spiritual energy, than it is to understand that we are God, or are one with God, although, that is truth.

The word God means so many different things to different people. It's important to have a definition of God that you're comfortable with. I hope you can see yourself as a divine being of good. It's an important concept to grasp as you begin to do this work.

If you consider that the real you is your soul or spirit, the highest part of you, the definition makes sense. It is our ego that doesn't want to accept the word 'God.' Ego thinks of God as having complete control over every one and every thing and, of course, ego doesn't want to relinquish its illusion of control.

Now we can substitute the idea of 'coming into alignment' for the somewhat more difficult term 'surrender', which for some implies giving up power or control. Alignment means to be in a position of agreement or alliance. When we align our soul/spirit with God/Spirit, the relationship is mutual, reciprocal; it is not giving your self up. When Jesus dictated this to me, it was a real epiphany for me...a real 'A-ha' moment. We have been programmed to believe that surrender has a strong negative connotation. I hope that now you can see that in the spiritual sense, surrendering to God/Spirit and aligning ourselves with God/Spirit, is the most positive and natural thing we can do.

It's inspiring to realize that there is a divine being that is mutually interested in our success in all areas of our life. Doesn't it make sense for us to seek out this relationship, to try to align our selves with that being, our soul and our soul's parent?

Unfortunately, in our society the very idea of God has taken on a negative connotation. Many people have given up on God because they have suffered disappointments and misery in their lives. If they see God as being 'in control,' they then struggle to understand how a divine being of good that is loving, compassionate and in control would allow bad things to happen to them or others.

I wouldn't even know where to begin to try to answer these questions, for I cannot. However, if we truly seek, find, and develop an intimate relationship with God we come to understand this relationship and knowledge differently. When we come into alignment and experience a personal relationship with God/Spirit we understand that God/Spirit does not turn away from us. It is we who turn away. We run away. We blame and deny there is such a loving spirit because we don't truly understand the unconditional love or how to receive it. Yet, it is what we all are craving, unconditional love. It is not available outside of us, yet this is where we seek it.

God/Spirit is only interested in a one-on-one relationship with you. It is up to you to do the seeking. That is what your journey on earth is about. Spirit is always present in our hearts. We just need to clear away the clutter to get to it. The more you allow your programing and society's programing to interfere with your journey, you lose out on knowing all the love and gifts that are awaiting you, and the gift that you truly are.

This is the hardest work you will ever have to do, but the benefits are priceless. You will keep bumping up against feelings of guilt and shame and patterns that act as a wedge keeping you from connecting with God/Spirit and accepting your worthiness and divinity.

Most of us carry so much guilt and shame because of our programing, and that includes programing about the concept of sin. If we feel sinful/guilty or unworthy it keeps us from getting close to God/Spirit. Remember, we are projecting everything about ourselves onto others, including God/Spirit. If we are judging our selves unworthy then we are projecting that God/Spirit will see us that way as well.

There is no truth to this at all. You are looked upon as holy (sacred) and there is no judgment because there is no such thing as right, wrong, or sin, we are guiltless. When we believe we are right or better than others we are still judging our self on a sin scale. 'I am not as sinful as that one.' This idea or belief about sin will keep you from truly understanding that God does not judge you. You are holy (sacred) and loved. As you learn to accept God's/Spirits love, your shame and guilt becomes less of a barrier to building your intimate relationship with God/Spirit.

Points to Ponder

- What is your definition of God/Spirit? Or your Higher Self?
- What thoughts or feelings arise when I talk about having a personal directly connected relationship with God/Spirit or your Higher Self for that matter?
- Does alignment or alliance help create a mutual relationship with God/Spirit versus surrendering?

Chapter Fourteen

You are Holy (sacred), God/Spirit is Holy, You are God, God is You

❀ ❀ ❀ ❀ ❀ ❀ ❀ ❀ ❀ ❀ ❀ ❀

Why do we need to bring ourselves
to the brink of devastation
when all we need to do is ask the divine self
that resides within for help.
We already have an internal compass
for every area of our life.
We do not have to wait until
desperation sets in.

❀ ❀ ❀ ❀ ❀ ❀ ❀ ❀ ❀ ❀ ❀ ❀

We are all sacred divine beings of goodness. It is our ego that believes the opposite. It is easy for the ego to control you if it makes you feel sinful, guilty, or shameful. The ego's job is to get you to fall in line so it can control you and keep you safe. It doesn't believe you're already safe and it never will.

Your soul/spirit knows you are safe and holy and that there is no such thing as sin. Our ego believes in sin due to programming. It creates storylines, dramas, entitlements, self-destructive patterns and all kinds of violence that we act out on others and/or on our self. It believes we are sinful, and it feels the need to hide our sin or blame others for our sinfulness.

If I told you there is no such thing as sin and that there are just thinking errors and poor judgments based on your ego's storyline, would that take away the feeling of guilt, shame and unworthiness?

The truth is, we just make thought or action errors as a result of decisions or understandings based on our ego's programing. If you can accept this as true, it will bring a huge shift in your understanding of life and who you really are. You'll cease carrying around all of that heavy emotional baggage about yourself and others. Remember, all that emotional weight affects us physically, emotionally and spiritually.

We need to stop believing in sin. It separates us from our spirit and from God. Our ego, family and society programed us to believe in the concept of sin. No one is to blame. It's part of your awakening to understand that what you learn in the outside world has little or no truth to it. If you don't keep digging for answers through a personal relationship with God, you can never learn the truth about anything. It is everyone's job or task to seek truth from within. If you are in alliance with God/Spirit, if you are in a mutual relationship of adoration, then wisdom will come. It is waiting for you to embrace it.

Imagine how much everyone has suffered by believing they are sinful and that God/Spirit thinks them unworthy. Our spirit/soul does not sin. It is only our ego that makes errors in judgment and thinking. It's heartbreaking to know that so many of us, including myself, have believed so much un-truth for so long. It keeps us in pain, alone and feeling lost.

But we aren't lost. We're just disconnected from the truth because we refuse or don't know how to connect to God/Spirit; it is like a delusion. When we let go of the delusion of believing the untruth about ourselves we are then healed. Through the awakening process we struggle with letting go of the delusion, it is part of the spiritual journey. Our patterns keep us entrenched in believing the delusion. Even if we get a glimpse of the truth, we forget and believe in the delusion again. This happens over and over and over again until we let go of the delusion totally. We would rather believe the worst about ourselves and others than accept the truth of perfection. If we are disconnected from God/Spirit, we are disconnected from our selves. Remember, we are Spirit, we are sacred, we are one with God. This disconnect is the cause of all the grief, suffering and despair that we don't want to feel, see, or know.

When we are disconnected from our soul/spirit, we try to fill ourselves with 'things' from the outside world to fill the void of emptiness within and to distract us and numb our pain. We become the living dead, living unfulfilled lives, or making believe we are happy and passionate when we're really filled with despair, aloneness, disconnection, separateness, fear and grief. We're spiritually asleep and unconscious and don't understand what we are doing, but we don't have to live unfulfilled, empty, spiritless lives.

It's time to wake up! There are many enlightened souls in this world that have found their way to God/ Spirit and have written books or developed programs to help you. There are many paths to enlightenment, including religion. There is no right or wrong way. The important thing is to discover what works for you, what you feel comfortable with. The only thing that matters is that you are doing the work and going inside to find truth.

There is no perfect way to do this. Our spirit is perfect; our ego is not. We are human; we make mistakes. The process will not look perfect to you through your ego's eyes. Ego will find fault with everything you do. Ego will make you feel as though you will never be good enough. Don't believe it! You are perfect. You are right where you should be. Take life one day at a time, one year at a time. Your soul/spirit will lead the way if you allow it to. Always have hope.

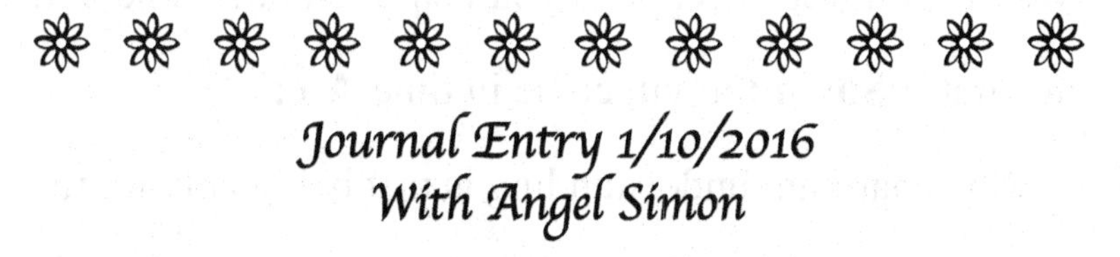

Journal Entry 1/10/2016
With Angel Simon

Simon: Good Morning my darling. We are here with you. We love you. What is your will today Deb? **Me:** To do God's will, although my ego says to pack and clean is my will (we were in the midst of moving). **Simon:** Interesting, I am glad that you can separate them. Today is to be holy. **Me:** Please clarify, what does that mean? **Simon:** To stay in God's spirit, to delight in awe of your life and what there is around you, to drink in love and beauty, to bestow your love onto others, to share the scripture of heaven.

Me: What is the scripture of heaven? **Simon:** It is to heal and be blessed through the love of God and all that is His. Everything is His, Debbie. All the people living in the world and everything in it living and not living are all one with God/Spirit. Yes, this includes eternity, past, present and future, the pulse of energy that surrounds everything. **Me:** This is very deep, can you help me understand and integrate? **Simon:** It will come in time. **Me:**

So, what I am understanding is that being holy means I need to stay connected to His love and purpose and all that God stands for. This would be having gratitude for the blessings of my life, that I am alive and all the abundance I have. To be happy, joyful and honor everything in my life, that there is so much that I have been honored with, family, friends, career, things/home, nature, myself and the gifts within me. **Simon:** Yes, that is beautiful!

Points to Ponder

- What role does shame, guilt or sin fit into your life?
- Are you constantly judging yourself?
- What thoughts or feelings arise when I tell you: 'You are holy, sacred and perfect?'
- What is your understanding about the delusion of unworthiness?
- Do you long for a deeper relationship with your higher self, the God within you?

Chapter Fifteen

Where Should I Be?

Life is not just something that you live
It is coursing through every cell in your body.
You are energy. You are life.

There are many levels of awakening and consciousness. Your growth depends on how much time you are willing and able to put into doing your spiritual work. We are all on our own journey and we are not all on the same level of consciousness or healing.

If you are reading this, you are already awakened to the truth that there is something more to you or life. You probably don't see it clearly or, if you do, you don't think you are far enough along on your path to consciousness. We all tend to believe that we need to keep moving on to higher levels of consciousness before we have integrated what we already learned. Our ego is still alive and well and telling us that we are flawed and imperfect and in need of additional healing quickly. We do need to heal from hurts. The ego's deception is having us believe that we are flawed and broken.

Our ego can't accept that our healing has already occurred and that we are right where we're supposed to be, unflawed and not broken. Ego can't and won't believe it. It tells us there must be something more we need to do to grow or be healed. This is the delusion, it is very strong and feels very real.

The reality is that you are soul, you are spirit, you are perfect as you are. Even though we have finally started to awaken from our unconscious story, our ego still has us caught up in our storyline, it's patterns, delusions and illusions. We have spent years believing and hiding the delusions. It takes a substantial amount of inner work with spirit to let go of this belief system.

We keep repeating the awakening and healing process and then rejecting the fact that we never needed to be healed in the first place. Then we forget again and our ego takes over and starts the loop all over again, and again, and again. The loop isn't broken until all the wisdom is fully integrated and we understand that we are fully healed, not believing the delusion anymore.

We have trouble accepting that life is an illusion, that we have been asleep and unconscious and living a storyline that we agreed on prior to our birth. It's all so difficult to grasp, because our ego can't make sense of it. It's even harder to hold on to it once we've grasped it!

As we engage in our day-to-day lives we are in our illusions and delusions along with everyone else. We are living our lives based on our storyline, like an actor in a play or movie, a character in a book.

Your awakening is recognizing there is no truth to the story. This is not your story. It is not who you are. It is a dream. It is a role you have been playing based on your illusion of life, your experiences and programing. It is a dream that we have difficulty wakening from. We wake up for a moment and fall back asleep. When we fall back asleep, we keep getting drawn back into believing the illusion. We still believe that we need to be healed from the brokenness and programing. So we keep working diligently seeking deeper levels of healing to attain deeper levels of consciousness.

This cycle will continue until you finally understand you are pure spirit/soul, you are not broken and never were; you were just unconsciously creating pain. I still get stuck in this cycle at times; it is a normal progression for those who are seeking.

This realization brings great freedom and joy. You can finally just be you. You no longer look at yourself or others in the same way as before. You don't need to prove yourself or get approval from the outside world. You don't need to hide your 'sins' or your untruths. You are plugged into the truth of life, aligned with God/Spirit, and you understand your purpose and recognize your gifts. You are awake and present and understand the role of the ego.

We are often surprised when we finally recognize what our gift is. It might be something that you never thought was in you or something you thought you had no skill for. But there it is, and it is divine.

You no longer feel lost, alone, or full of grief. Your life becomes purposeful and full of light. You want to share this light and purpose with others. It feels right and you are passionate about it. You can't help the immediacy you feel about doing this. Nothing else in your life felt more right than this because it is coming from your heart through your spirit and it fulfills and nurtures your soul.

Don't question why, what or how. You'll intuitively know that you were meant to share your gifts and your purpose with the rest of the world. You are being called to inspire others. It is what you are here to do. Embrace it. It is a blessing and so are you.

Jesus: Tell me what you are thinking. **Me:** That I now realize that everything I've experienced in life, my husband, my children, and what happened when I was younger was simply a dream, and that because there is a certain collective consciousness of souls, we all participate and take part in each other's dreams. **Jesus:** Yes, we had this discussion before and it was hard to understand. **Me:** So I did not suffer abuse? **Jesus:** It was part of the dream you believed was true. **Me:** So nothing really happened? **Jesus:** No.

Me: That seems crazy! What a waste of time and energy to suffer something like that and then come to understand that it never really happened. **Jesus:** It is, I agree, but it is part of your soul's lessons. Are you done with suffering? **Me:** I would very much like to be. **Jesus:** Good, then we can start with creating the life that you want here on earth! **Me:** Okay, I would like that. What do we do? **Jesus:** Stop doing. **Me:** What do you mean? **Jesus:** You feel like you need to keep doing to make it happen but it is already done. **Me:** So, I just need to wait for it to start? **Jesus:** It already has, you have already been noticing all the blessings, they will just continue. Just enjoy it, do the things that you want to do, that you love to do, have fun. Creating should be fun. What do you want to create? **Me:** Love, peace, beauty, awakening. I thought we were writing a book to help people awaken, love themselves and others, heal what people believe need to be healed, although my understanding is that nothing is true about that. What an amazing book "Our Illusion"! What about the aches and pains I have? **Jesus:** Bodies do breakdown Deb, it is part of being human. **Me:** But what about healing our bodies; why can't that be part of the illusion or use of our power to do it? **Jesus:** We do have the power to heal ourselves. **Me:** So how do I get rid of my psoriasis? **Jesus:** Believe you can. **Me:** Believe I can? What about my finger, toe, liver, hair? **Jesus:** Yes, all of it. Believe that you are completely healed, because you are, everything will regenerate to its healthy point in time. **Me:** I need more help with all of this. I need clarity. I know I need to stop resisting the truth. I remember when you first told me that life was a dream, that I believed things happened to me and that I experienced them fully, and this was so difficult to understand. I felt like it was time to wake up and understand more but I didn't know how to feel about what I was learning. It was very difficult to wrap my head around the idea that all my experiences are like dreams or nightmares, that they didn't really happen, that I don't carry scars that need to be healed, and that there is nothing wrong with me or anyone else other than what we perceive about ourselves. Now I understand why the idea that we are sinless and guiltless is so very important. It would be very difficult to accept that life is filled with such untruth. It would take the meaning of everything away that we work so hard to apply meaning to. So I understand how one can go from the idea that "nothing really matters" when you first begin to see the illusion of life, to the realization that "everything matters", because you now understand the true meaning, purpose and beauty of everything that surrounds you. It hurts to know that most of the planet, including myself, does not understand this and they are living in pain rather than bliss. There is so much unnecessary pain everywhere, but I guess it is necessary to process our soul's lessons. If you do not recognize it is a dream you hold onto everything as if it is real. What a complexity! So all I have to do is enjoy, take care of human business because it is how the world of earth works, allow my dream to manifest by creating and being the purpose I am here for. I needed to wake up from the nightmares and wonderful dream of my life to realize they are all just a dream. I needed to see the beauty in everything, get rid of the old stories, heal the negative patterns so I can just be love and creativity. I am so grateful for this gift of clarity and light Jesus.

Points to Ponder

- How much time do you put into a spiritual practice?
- Where do you feel you are in your growth?
- Are you awakening and then forgetting? What are you forgetting?

The next part of your spiritual

journey will be found in Volume 3

Expanding Your World View

See you there, I'll be waiting for
you with more love……

Printed in the United States
By Bookmasters

Printed in the United States
By Bookmasters